STARMAN

MY LIFE AND AFTERLIFE

JOANNE HELFRICH

Author of *Afterlives: Firsthand Accounts of Twenty Notable People*

NEWWORLDVIEW

Illustrations incorporate original images used
under license from Shutterstock.com.
Special thanks to Intueri

First Printing: June 2023
ISBN: 978-0-9828123-9-6

10 9 8 7 6 5 4 3 2 1

*For all you pretty things, driving
your Mamas and Papas insane,
making way for Homo Superior*

There's a starman waiting in the sky
He'd like to come and meet us
But he thinks he'd blow our minds
There's a starman waiting in the sky
He's told us not to blow it
'Cause he knows it's all worthwhile
He told me
Let the children lose it
Let the children use it
Let all the children boogie

- David Bowie

A playlist for your journey –
all songs by David Bowie

Space Oddity

Changes

Oh! You Pretty Things

Life On Mars?

Soul Love

Moonage Daydream

Starman

Hang Onto Yourself

Ziggy Stardust

Suffragette City

Rock 'n' Roll Suicide
(You're Not Alone)

Young Americans

Somebody Up There Likes Me

Heroes

Blackstar

Lazarus

I Can't Give Everything Away

— *Introduction by Joanne Helfrich —*

I'm a channeler, which is similar to a medium. One of my gifts is the ability is to communicate with people who are no longer physical, but are quite alive in an afterdeath state.

You might wonder, *exactly how is this done*? I start with a heartfelt desire to help people. Then I ask specific questions to a specific no-longer-physical person. I place my hands on my computer keyboard and go into a conscious trance state — aware but detached — and allow my fingers to intuitively move across the keys. Using my inner senses, I receive letters, words, and sentences. Sometimes I receive concepts that I can't put into words until my fingers do.

The process is supported by other helpful spiritual energies. My very wide, knowledgeable, go-to spirit guide, Rose, describes the process as a collaboration between me and the *worldview* of the person in the afterdeath state who exists as they were *and more*, incorporating their own greater Selves, or souls. Rose, having knowledge of them, helps translate their energy into a form I can receive. You might think of Rose as a multidimensional radio transmitter and me the radio who tunes into each person's "station".

After completing my previous book, *Afterlives* — featuring twenty notable people no longer physical — I wondered, *who will I speak with next? What will I ask?*

STARMAN

Afterlives is exceptional in its ability to connect readers with twenty beloved, no-longer-physical geniuses. Even if I could do it again, I wasn't sure I wanted to. *Afterlives* provides so much wisdom, and so many wonderful moments, that another book like it seemed unnecessary.

I contemplated this for a year. Then I realized that what I wanted to know more about were the many soulful, spiritual things that often aren't considered that—art, music, creativity, sex, drugs, and rock and roll. In my view, all these things can be considered spiritual when approached that way. I realized that a book like it was overdue—one that would challenge assumptions about what is and isn't spiritual, open up our creative apertures, and provide an informed view of the deeper nature of reality. It certainly would have helped me during my early adulthood in the rough and rocky 1970s!

So one morning in December 2022, I asked Mr. David Bowie—one of my generation's greatest artists—to collaborate on this book. His views on all of the above topics, and his many creative explorations while physical—including fluidity of style and sexuality—make him an important artist for these times, too. He's helped millions of us consider many different, freeing ideas, in contrast to the limiting ones we've been raised with.

Starman

My feeling was then, as it is now, that *we need Mr. Bowie now as much as ever*. I also felt he might enjoy the opportunity to continue his work while on the other side, as many of my previous authors have done with enthusiasm.

Did he write this book? I know *I* didn't, nor could I. As you'll discover, it was written from the perspective of a wise, caring gentleman who shares his experiences from his physical life and beyond it. He identifies himself as Starman. I believe Starman includes the worldview of Mr. Bowie — as he was and more, incorporating his own greater Self, or soul.

Starman wants to help us to be whole and embrace the vast, magical reality we are part of, as he has.

What better advice is there for those he addresses directly — young people — and every one of us needing to recognize *soul* in art, sex, identity, and other forms of expression? And what greater thing than to help guide and inspire those who are coming of age during one of the most profoundly turbulent periods in history? Given these are themes explored by Mr. Bowie while physical, it's hard to imagine that he wouldn't want to help write this book. Its messages are consonant with his fantastic music, which I highly recommend listening to.

Mr. Bowie also seemed, while physical, to have been creatively inspired by other "psychological aspects" that existed beyond his own physical reality. It stands to reason that he continues to do that on his nonphysical journey, and that he would reach back into physical reality to help us do the same. This book and all my books are evidence that this is possible.

Who's to say that each of us isn't creatively influenced by psychological aspects other than what we consider "our own"? This might be at the very heart of the creative process—and a big part of our physical experience—whether or not we recognize it. Starman is saying, "be open to whatever positive, loving inspiration you can and make yourself your own work of art," which is what Mr. Bowie has always done, too.

You might be wondering, *how is this even possible*? The idea to keep in mind is that everything is conscious in our physical world and beyond it. Postmodern science is starting to understand that *consciousness is the unified field of everything*, and we are all connected to everyone and everything, *ever*. This idea is further discussed in this book.

Perhaps it's not important who wrote this book but whether or not it is valuable. I hope it is for you, and that you enjoy this amazing, Cosmic journey!

Joanne Helfrich
Topanga, California
June 2023

STARMAN

— *And now, Starman* —

I didn't know this thing was ready for me when I was dying—this *thing*—this miraculous ability to find me in space then transcend multiple layers of consciousness to speak with me—this daring, useful, totally amazing thing that's happening here.

I just have to say, "good work," you writer of things needing to be said, though you're not the one saying them. I'm grateful.

When I say *dying*, I mean that the way in which I chose to depart was somewhat intuited by me, David, without much thought about it.

Then it became an ingenious way to categorize my existence. What would I leave? What would I take with me? This was the last thing I would ever do. What would it be like? What would I take into account, without bothering too much about whatever the current situation was I was in?

There were loved ones. There were many loved ones who wanted my good health, of course. I wasn't able to give them that. I was much more equanimous about the outcome than they were. I was justified in my ability to say "this is fine" because I really did mean it. This was something I would enjoy, in a sense. So I did.

I enjoyed my passing. I enjoyed the archetypal sorts of thoughts about death, the resurrection towards the Self I would become, this self I would definitely call my Self in the *whole* sense. I was more than I was even when alive on Earth.

I was more, even, when I was a baby. There was something to me that was different, I sense, now that I'm here, beyond the physical reality I was part of.

I'm more than the billions of stars. How's that for a reckoning?

Where did I leave off in my existence — beyond the skeletal remains — and where did I end up? In the stars? The heavens? Are they above, or below, where I am?

I knew full well I would become what I became. Let's just say for now that I'm the Starman that you knew I was when physical. Now I'm just that without a body. You can think of me this way.

I'm the Starman.

STARMAN

STARMAN

Now, onto the specifics of my demise.

The world was in a state of ignorance. The world has been in a state of ignorance for millions of years, in some ways, but the last thirty to fifty years on the planet for me were utterly banal in so many ways.

There were many ways to achieve greater art, though, and this was what I put much of my energy into, though I was able to also put to rest many of the personas I'd created and settle into a life of comfort as a father and husband.

The stress of life, therefore, was nonexistent for me, in many ways, towards the end of my life. But there were also, still, the forces that were not helping people, and so many things to say, so many things to do with regard to helping people see the greater reality they live in.

I knew then—and I know now even more than before—that the world is blind to what's really going on.

✦

This is what I strived to say in my work — *that there are many ways to see the world* — and I was there to show them as many of them that I could — Ziggy Stardust, Major Tom, Aladdin Sane, the Pierrot clown, the Thin

White Duke, the charismatic speaker, the alternatives I shared with regard to dressing in ways that brought a certain fluidity of style between genders.

These were all things I wanted to say then. I wanted to scream them sometimes, too.

Then I realized the world was also in need of love, care, compassion. These became what I needed to share, too.

✦

I loved whoever came into my path, and I was able to correct a lot of their thinking about themselves, because people realized they were beautiful, too, in spite of how they were brought up to believe. And while I was able to help correct some of the thinking about themselves, I was also able to correct the ways in which they chose to do some things rather than others.

I was able to show the world what it was in so many ways. The vapid, sexless landscape of culture was something I chose to take on as a form of protest, but a protest that was foremost my own work of art.

The art was the tool I used to help transform hearts into ones that realized the joy in the music of the time, and the forms of sexuality and belonging and dress and other forms of expression that I brought into awareness. This was—above all—*my own* quest for truth and beauty, and it took hold all around the world.

And when your realize what a capable person I *was*, then you can get a sense of who I am *now, again*.

I want to show you all what it is to be whole.

I want to show you what awaits you beyond this life.

I want to show you whatever you need to see, because *I'm in your thoughts now* and I want you to know what you really are to me.

You're a Starman, too. You just don't realize it yet.

I was born in the streets, in a sense. There were many wonderful things about my childhood, but I will always remember being in the streets with my mates, my friends.

This was sometimes combative, of course, and this was also the most wonderful time because I had a lot of fun. I had friends beyond my neighborhood, too. These would be the best friends I could hope for. You have these kinds of friends, too. The more friends you have, the better, because you never can know what awaits you when a friend calls.

To open the door to friendship is about the best way to go into the world every day. The world will help you find people to be with.

I was a big advocate of this, and I shed a lot of tears from betrayals, too, but I was even more enriched by friends who cared about me. This offset the pain from those who wished me ill. I had these people just like you do.

You see me as a rock star, too, but you have to realize I was as human as you are, and I was not perfect, and I had a lot of issues, too. These include addiction, some degree of betrayal of others, and, more importantly, some issues with not caring enough about people.

I have to show you this side of me so you know that I'm as human as anybody... still, in some ways.

So don't ever feel like I'm here telling you this because I'm beyond this. I still suffer from some things. That's what makes me whole.

And I will say this, too: you will be whole when you're able to see yourself as somebody who *does their best.* You *don't* have to be *perfect.* You only need to show yourself some compassion sometimes. Then keep going forward, being open to new experiences, people, and whole sets of extraordinary things that will come your way if you let them. That's what I've done.

And I will say, too, that the reasons for my wanting to say this are to help you, because I was helped when I was living, and it's important to help others when you can. You can't get more basic than the basic rule to do unto others as you want people to behave towards you.

The funny thing is that I find myself sounding a bit like an old uncle, passing along all the things he wishes he'd known sooner and doesn't mean to intrude but can't help himself for wanting to help.

This is sort of odd to say, perhaps, but while I tend to tell people what to do, I really do want to sit back and watch you take charge of your life. And I will.

There are some things, though, that I feel strongly about you knowing, because the world is so very odd right now and I have to shed light on things so you can judge for yourself and let go of your fears about what others tell you, mostly.

✦

I wasn't really a great student because I was constantly wanting to go out and play with my friends.

You might consider this, too, to get you out of the thinking that you have to figure things out on your own. You don't. Sometimes friends give perspectives that you have never realized are true, so let them.

So I enjoyed my friendships a lot when I was living. I was able to broker a sort of peace between people, too, that helped me be a trusted friend. You don't have to take sides. You just need to find a way to say, "this person feels this way" and "that person feels this way" without judging what they should be doing.

Stay neutral. This will help you a lot.

The way in which the world pits people against each other is wrong. This kind of fomenting of conflict between people is used as a means to drive a wedge between people.

Don't let that happen, even in your small circle of intimate friends. You won't be able to replace people when you lose them. I found that out the hard way.

The purpose of my saying all of this is that you have a lot of comrades waiting to be friends with you, you just haven't met them yet. When you do, be honest about what you like and don't like. You don't have to like all the same things. You only have to get along with what the other person likes.

The reasons, therefore, for having a lot of friends is to expand your horizons, to think differently about some things sometimes. You don't have to always agree.

Just take your time with people. Be there for them as best you can. However, when things go in a bad direction, you also need to ensure you allow them to take their leave without begging them to stay. There's sometimes need to let go of friendships. Just be sure to realize what you have learned, then be on your way.

The reason I'm talking about friendships is because I was a lot of fun when I was around friends. You can be this, too. Be fun with people. Have fun being silly, funny, outrageous. If you can't do this around your friends, when can you?

This has been about the best thing in my life, this ability to be courageous with my friends. This of course made me outrageous on stage.

Do you see how this happened? I turned my courageous outlandishness into a way to entertain. Then I was able to move beyond this into new realms of experience.

So begin with finding friends you can be yourself around, then let go of the fears about expressing yourself outrageously. Kindly, though. Not harming. Just effectively.

The reason I want to shed light on my life is to help you with yours.

The friendships were important.

STARMAN

My family, too, has been important to me. The mates — the spouses, that is — I had were those who were able to see what I needed, then to allow me to be who I would be, giving what they could to help me along my way.

This is true for everybody, I think, the need to find marriages and partnerships that will be productive in the sense of mutual satisfaction.

The needs you have are real. You need food, water, shelter, love, caring, success in your work. These are things others can help you with. But a mate — a life partner or spouse — will help you more than friends in some regards and having this coexistence can be very helpful.

You don't have to. However, for me it was a very important thing to be married when I was. The first marriage I entered into was fully due to convenience, so there was not any romantic love there or that kind of thing. However, there was appreciation on both sides, and many benefits that came from the partnership, including the birth of my son. My second marriage was more fulfilling in every way, and my daughter a gift in my older years.

✦

This can be the same for you. The world is a big place. You can find love in the sense of partnerships to help you. This has become a way to sometimes throw shadows on others, though. You don't need to have the best-looking person. You need to have the person you see as beautiful, and to do this you need to be open-hearted.

Too many people are alone because of a paucity in use of one's heart to discern what is right for them. I don't want you to do this. I want you to embrace every person you can, then see what kind of benefit they will have for you. Someone will be the one you need to be whole in your life. Then let them.

The reality of life is that there are so many rotten institutions that punish people for being who they are.

When you allow this into your thinking, too, you punish people. You tend to allow only the beautiful, strong people into your life, or those who would be considered popular, then you ignore people who really have something more to offer.

You might instead try letting everyone in, then kick out anybody who is unkind person. There's not any reason to allow a bully to threaten you or anybody you love.

✦

There were a lot of songs I put together in pieces, literally cutting up pieces of paper in order to mix up words in ways that you never would have imagined, which is why this random method suited me so well.

This was fun, too, and it showed in the songs. I was able to randomize the words in ways that were fun but telling as well.

The instruments were added to punch things up, so things were never dull, always exciting. The ideas sometimes got mixed together in really innovative ways, too. This wasn't more striking, perhaps, as it was in my song "Suffragette City," which now seems old-fashioned compared to how loose things have gotten sexually.

However, there's a glint of irony in the way I put together the ideas. The suffragette in the song was about a woman who was sexually free, while the same policy of freedom might be applied to the original suffragettes, woman who fought for the rights of women to vote. This was odd in a moral as well as liberating way, which is one reason I think the song had so much power to it.

This is the kind of thing that embraced me, this kind of "suffragette city" mentality that had everybody screaming about how beautiful the song was but failed to see that the suffragette was the one who was up against the hierarchy that was keeping everybody down.

The suffragettes were not only fighting for *women's* rights—they were fighting for *everybody's* rights. They were fighting for decency, for average people, for the lives of everybody who ever lived.

And when I made that song, this was a grappling way to say, "This is not exactly what you think the song is about." This was not understood by many. I was paying homage to them, not belittling them.

✦

So I'm saying this now: *you need to stand up for people.* You need to get this into your thinking every single day because the world needs you to do this.

I was somebody who complained only about the people who kept others down. This was my only complaint.

There were so many ways this was done during my lifetime. There were elements at play in banking and other financial institutions, in the power brokers, the oligarchs, the mad hatters in the stock market.

The many reasons for saying "fuck you" to these people were in some ways what I strove to do. The songs were reflections that were not really about them, exactly. They were deeper, more subtle ways to inflict upon them many people who trusted themselves to be indignant or flamboyant when they needed to be.

Outrageous would be the best word to describe what I was going for. I think I succeeded.

✦

When I was a child, I was drawn to music, especially that which I could play on my own. The way I went about trying out instruments was to pick one up and give it a try. I recommend this for anyone, because you never know what you'll be able to play until you try it. I loved every instrument, but the recorder was the first one I could hold in my hands and generate my own music. This was a huge love right from the beginning.

Writing was second. I liked to write as a boy, and I was able to sometimes write little songs without caring much about what they were about. This was a habit I continued because I didn't care much about what things were about. I wanted to *affect* things, not *preach*.

So I would argue that sometimes people think too much about what they want to say without needing much effort to say it. But what they miss is that you really don't need to be certain about what you want to say. You just need to say it.

This is something I want you to do. Just say what's on your mind without being certain about anything.

This is what I did all the time. I was about to be wholly given to anything at the time without needing to feel something like certainty about it. This was a "forest for the trees" situation. I was able to see the forest for the trees without needing to specify which tree, which forest, etc.

Just allow yourself to not be certain, that's all.

✦

The prognosis for the world is this: you will be fine, you will not be fine. These are two contradictory statements that I want you to cherish in your heart because this is exactly the issue: you will be fine, you will not be fine.

Now what do I mean by this? Heaven awaits you. That's for sure.

That's what I'm finding now in this state of afterdeath, this wonderful place here. All things are equal, loving, potentiated in so many ways that you may need to put on sunglasses, for the lights are so bright with choices that you will need to turn down the wattage.

The life you have now is about the best one you can imagine, which is something you need to hear. The way your life has been so far is about the best way you can consider because it's made exactly for you.

How can this be? Because the energetic patterns of life are exactly where they need to be *for you only*, for *you solo*, for *you* dear reader.

Everything is whole and you're a part of it.

Where can you go from here besides into more satisfying places?

Indeed the effort you've put towards your own ability to have a good time while on planet Earth has paid off. You've gotten about the best experiences you could ever hope for.

What do I mean? If you think about this, where else would you learn about being a soul than good old planet Earth?

Why venture beyond Earth if what you really needed all along is right here?

In fact, I would swear by this if I had the ability to do so. I don't now because there's nothing cast in concrete. Everything is in a state of possibility, so it's entirely possible there are better worlds for you right now. However, I haven't seen any yet.

So your life is one big, impossible, subjective experience that can only be considered Divine when you realize the world is exactly as you, my dear reader, have made it.

The reason I say this is because you create your own reality — all of it — and you do so because you are gods in the making. You have all the tools ready to be employed to make yourself a better, more mature and capable person. That's why life throws so many things at you: so you can learn how to be more than you ever thought you could.

Everything about your life has its unique challenges, made especially for you. The fit is always going to be exactly as you need it to be: too big, too small, too rich, too poor, too manic, too calm, too this and that.

✦

The world is you, and if you can just take a deep breath sometimes and see how very lucky you have been to be part of this creation, you will realize this.

Try to do this now: *breathe the world.*

Do you see how very beautiful the world is? Do you see yourself as part of it? If you don't, you need to, because life is going to pass you very quickly and it would be good if you were to take a bit of it as it wooshes by.

The reason for writing this book is to help people who have a lot of energy without, necessarily, a great place to share it. This is in some ways due to how you've been brought up to believe that you're supposed to do things in ways that are not fun or interesting. I want to relieve you of this burden so you can see this differently.

The way I want you to think about life is as a giant painting that you can make into whatever you want.

You can write, draw, paint, do things musical, anything that takes you out of the commonplace into the kind of painting that you want to be in. The painting is the creative world that you want to invent to help yourself and others be happy.

This is doable when you realize that the way the world works is sometimes not the way you necessarily want to.

✦

This is how you can get to doing the painting of your life. First... *see yourself as the hero of your own life.*

This means taking everything in as it comes to you, then doing the best you can with it. This doesn't mean jumping into burning buildings. This is about trying to do your best to help yourself and others each day you're alive.

Because when it comes right down to it, this is the *reason* for life: to help yourself and others without caring much sometimes if you're really able to. You just need to try.

The next point is to *try to be a friend to others.* This means the people in your life — if you can. However, the way the world works is that when you're open to new experiences, you'll find your friends along the way.

So be easy to get along with, and the friends you want to have in your life will appear miraculously sometimes. Be open to that.

The next thing is to *trust that you have a lot of brilliant things to talk about and share in whatever ways you feel like.*

These things are ways you can create the world you want to live in. Be sure to be kind when you're doing this, and you will be about the best artist of your world that you can be.

That's all I have to say about what kind of advice I want to give you, because you will find out for yourself.

✦

With that, I will now go onto where I think you really want to be with me, which is the afterlife. I will be sure to let you know in words — and in actions that you may notice in your everyday existence — that *this really is real.*

The afterlife is a lot like what you see each day you're alive. There are many ways to be in the world and even more ways in the afterlife. The thing is, you really will find out later on when you get here that the reasons for living are to be having fun where you are today, *now.*

You don't have to die to do what you feel like doing. In fact, you can't because the world will give you what you need even if things are tough sometimes. The world will not give you what you don't need. In this, we all have to face our sadness and challenges to move beyond where we are.

Therefore offing oneself — taking one's own life — has no reason to occur because *you will not escape from your problems*. The problems are needed for you to grow.

In other words, you need to change, and doing this is about the most remarkable thing you can do.

Given the many ways you see change happen in Nature, why would you — a creature of Nature — *also* not go through the kinds of metamorphoses that trees, birds, and butterflies do? You wouldn't be human.

If you don't *think* you have the ability to change, deep down you *know* you can.

I had a large amount of problems when I was physical.

I was a humble person, mostly, and I was not given to big celebrations about myself. Therefore, when I became a big rock star, I sometimes had trouble dealing with the attention. There was also too much to handle with regard to lovers, managers, and various duties that came with the role.

My inability to deal with my life was why I became addicted to drugs. This was not something I would do now, because I see that the reason for doing this was because I didn't feel like I was able to solve my problems.

The drugs became a *big* problem because they were a distraction from what I felt I had to do, which was sometimes make big decisions about the people who were in my life or things I needed to do better.

This is why I don't suggest doing drugs in quantities. These can be done in small amounts in order to enjoy yourself, but watch out, because these addictions are hard to kick, and I don't want to tell you otherwise.

✦

The way I see the reasons for my altered states is that I wanted to sometimes feel like I was in the presence of Something Greater, too, and people do this in ways that they think will bring them greater depth or joy. But this can't really happen when you only think of God or the Divine as something that's only there when you're in a state that's brought on by drugs.

Eventually you need to realize this "formless Divinity," let's say, is always around you. The way you can think about this is, you feel me now, right? I'm not God, certainly, but I represent something that's Divine about your reality.

This is something I was able to do on my own in real life, too. I was a very loving person. I was able to be a good parent. I was able to help many artists. And I as able to do this while physical.

Now I'm here to tell you this is the same here. You don't have to die to understand this: *please don't. You can get this right now*, which I will tell you about now.

✦

The way to participate in the things that are glorious in the world, the things that are Divine in every way, is to allow yourself to feel like a wonder-filled child, full of awe and reverence for everything around you.

You have a sense that many of the adults in charge have lost this, and you're right. You don't have to be like this. You can realize the world is always filled with wonder, and this is about as close to being God as I've ever seen.

I've seen a lot here and there—and I have to believe now—that the energy patterns that create reality are filled with love and that's the best kind of God you can ask for.

The God you think of as being mean isn't really God. God is Love. If you want to think about this differently, you might take my form of understanding, that is, the God you think of is everything in the world that's good.

So don't ever feel you're alone in the world without God.

Your form of God, or Divinity—or whatever you want to call it—is in each individual and in you, too.

Keep that in mind on your blue days.

STARMAN

The point of all this, of course, is to help you with your life.

I wasn't really that into being godlike. I was somebody who worshipped life in every way. I was able to move past the many kinds of things that people tie themselves up with, like bad marriages or bad jobs.

I was fluid in this way, being open to how things moved me. The classical music changed to pop, rock, blues, etc. These were all inspirations to me, this variety of music ideas, too. I had interest in reading many authors. The spiritual stuff wasn't really foremost on my list. This was something I felt rather than read a lot about.

I suggest you read as much as you can of books and things you're interested in and build your interests.

The more interests you have, the better.

✦

Tantamount to my view then, while physical, was also having fun musically, of course. The reason I say "musically" is that *everything* for me was musical, even the voices of those I loved. This was the reason I probably became a singer. I sang all the voices I loved.

The purpose for my life, therefore, was in seeing myself as a performer who could talk to anybody who was open to whatever self I portrayed.

The authors of books about me write about how I was able to swap identities flawlessly, but I was never always sure about what would "take" in people, what they would respond to.

I felt this strongly: these characters were real. *Really real.* The changes I went through—that happened when I created these characters—were the changes I needed to have myself go through.

For example, the Thin White Duke persona came at a time when I wasn't quite right with what the world was asking me. I was feeling a bit spent having toured quite a bit. I was also living the kind of aristocratic life of the rock star.

The Thin White Duke was me then, but the dual nature of his ability to portray *me* while I was portraying *him* was utterly fascinating for me. I was him onstage and, to some degree, in real life. He was me doing things he didn't usually do, for example, singing onstage and being a rock star. There were things he did that I wouldn't do and vice versa.

The way I see this is that I adopted an archetype that was somebody I needed to embody at that time, and he needed it, too. This is something of a challenge to explain but I'll try to do this now.

When you *see yourself as* a hero, you connect with energy that's going to help you *be* a hero.

You can think of a hero as somebody you love who is a good person, who does things for people. You might consider a girl who is a leader in her country standing up for her rights and the rights of others. Many people in your world today are this kind of hero.

There are also heroes you may have read about in history books — the founders of countries, the fighters of battles, the leaders of revolutions.

These are all somewhat different, yet they are all the same in some ways, too. They represent the hero archetype, which is something like a model of how to be. You can think of this as a spiritual being who is there to help you through whatever it is you need to do.

When you adopt the archetypical hero figure, you will feel strengthened by them. When you adopt the archetype of the holy person, you will be this, too. The thing to keep in mind is that each of these archetypes is just something that's helpful, not something to immerse yourself in. You need all of the archetypes to be whole. This means that you have to adopt the kind of feeling that I had when I was choosing different personas.

Personas are constant reinventions of ways to express archetypes in the world, which is important because archetypes require expression. My heroic impulses were always included in my personas. So you might say that the hero archetype was largely being expressed in a variety of ways.

The Thin White Duke was a persona who was somewhat closed off, a remote person who needed time to sort things out in comfort.

The Ziggy Stardust character was a flamboyant idol who wanted people to break out of their grey existence. I was him in some ways, too, because I was breaking out of this kind of world, too.

The way you can think about this is that you have many aspects to you. You don't have to be one way all the time. You can find personas to play with.

But keep in mind that these are personas only: they don't define all of you. And the reason this is important to realize is, you don't need to adopt them forever. They are to help you get through certain points in your life.

As I said, you need every archetype to be whole, in a sense. That's what I've found to be true here in the afterlife.

✦

There are still many personas for me to try on. But I have a sense I don't need to so much anymore because I've integrated them into my new Self. I'm more than David now.

I'm David Plus, you might say, having had the benefit of moving through a lot of things I've needed to in order to be where I'm at now. And I can rely on myself to find a way through my own experiences now without needing to adopt any one persona.

There are many kinds of ways to be.

I just want to help you move through things without caring too much about being one way or another.

Eventually, you need to put the personas aside like I did and metamorphose into the next you.

STARMAN

The way I like to think about myself now is as the White Duke with many lifetimes that make him more of a multicolored Self underneath the face.

That is to say, when I speak with you, I have to give you some semblance of David Bowie the way you knew me, but really I'm much more than that. I'm more than every lifetime I've ever lived, in some ways, while also being all of them, too.

This isn't as straightforward as you might think it is, as *the multidimensional world is real*.

Therefore, I exist in many lifetimes, probable dimensions, and the many things you've heard about me exploring these realities is true because I've always had an interest in it.

✦

The reason for sharing this with you is, you exist in many ways beyond this life, too.

You don't have to think, though, that you're in some ways incomplete because you don't realize what this is like. You can feel totally complete by just suggesting to yourself that the world really is on your side. The world was created in love and gives you everything you need.

This is something I will repeat now because I'd like for you to understand everything in the context of *other selves* who understand more about what you need sometimes than *you* might.

The world really is on your side. The world was created in love and gives you everything you need.

✦

The way to consider your multidimensional Self is as a giant iceberg with which the underwater portions are huge. The underwater—or invisible—part of yourself is about as big as an ocean. The underwater parts of yourself are also filled with love and information and all kinds of possibilities.

You exist in yourself as you are now—in your physical body—as the point of the iceberg that you can see. You can see other iceberg tops around you.

However, under the water there are vast spaces that go on forever and are filled with energy that goes on forever, too. That is to say, you're also part of this *vast* energy.

✦

This relates to how it's possible that I'm helping the woman typing these words to commit to your book the thoughts that will help *you* specifically. I'm here with you, too, as energy that's helpful. You have many other loving energies around you helping you, too.

The fact that I'm not physical is irrelevant. *I'm here with you in spite of what you think.*

This is also how I was able to transcend the world when physical, too. I had a lot of help from the nonphysical world. This is why I was able to do so many different things. I trusted who I was open to. I didn't allow anything in that was harmful to me, energetically speaking.

This is what I want you to do, too: trust only the loving energies around you to be helpful.

Let go of any fears about this being something unusual. It is in every way the same thing as your religions may teach you about angelic realms.

✦

I exist in a state of energy that's in many ways floating about helping others, the same way I was helped.

Isn't that what you feel is needed in your world? Isn't that what you might call inspiration? What exactly is inspiration if not for the whispers you hear within you that are helpful?

This is exactly what this book is doing: *helping you learn to listen to the whispers of spirit so you can be whole. It is helping you remember who you really are.*

The energy patterns I mentioned earlier have this all sorted out. The Universe is indeed well-organized and prone to helping those who need it towards areas of experience that will help them with whatever is required.

The world you live in is part of the Greater Scheme that supports everything that ever was.

In the case of my life, for example, the patterns were such that required me to emulate love in order to be who I needed to be. The world was accommodating of who I was in the sense of allowing me to do what I needed to do. I was aligned with the goodness of the world, and I was tapping into areas of consciousness that you can tap into, too.

In this, you have a wonderful opportunity to calmly move into new areas of wholeness and remind yourself of how very loved you have always been.

You are a part of everything that ever was.

So when you sometimes feel like you're alone, this is just an illusion. You're always with somebody who loves you. You're always with somebody who thinks you're wonderful. You're always with somebody who really wants you to be happy.

And when you think, "no this can't be," this is only because of how you were brought up to be constantly doubting everything good or magical in the world. *You don't need to believe this.*

The way to see yourself is as amazing and capable of doing amazing things if you would only let yourself. This is what I did, and you can do, too.

✦

Take stock of what you're good at, and what you think you need in order to get by, then find a way to blend the two in order to do work that's going to be fulfilling for you. If you can feel fulfilled with what you do each day, you will have about the most amazing life you can imagine.

The reason this is important is becoming more apparent every day.

Do you see how the world is changing?

Do you see how big empires are toppling because they don't have the decency to treat people well?

Do you see people fighting for the freedoms of themselves and others?

Do you see people fighting for the health of the planet and all of its creatures, plants, and peoples?

Do you know how very lucky you are to be living in a time when so many changes are happening?

This is about the most amazing time to be alive. This world is getting stronger in spite of what you might think sometimes.

When you think the world is going to hell, you really need to do something more to help yourself and others.

✦

What ways might you help relieve even the slightest bit of suffering in the world?

Doing something kind for somebody. Helping with duties around where you live, in your home or neighborhood. Being fit enough to carry groceries from the car, or walk the dog, to help others not have to do so much. Letting someone you love know you care about them. Seeing how you might help someone not feel so alone.

There are myriad things you can do to preserve the peace in your home. You might help resolve a conflict or preserve what's needed with regard to food or finances, or take time out to support somebody who needs to talk. Even just being friendly and in a good mood can go a long way in helping someone through their day.

There are so many things you can do daily to both help others and, in the process, to help yourself. You will feel better when you do.

Take action to do something to make the world a little better and you will feel better as result.

You will feel like the hero you need to be.

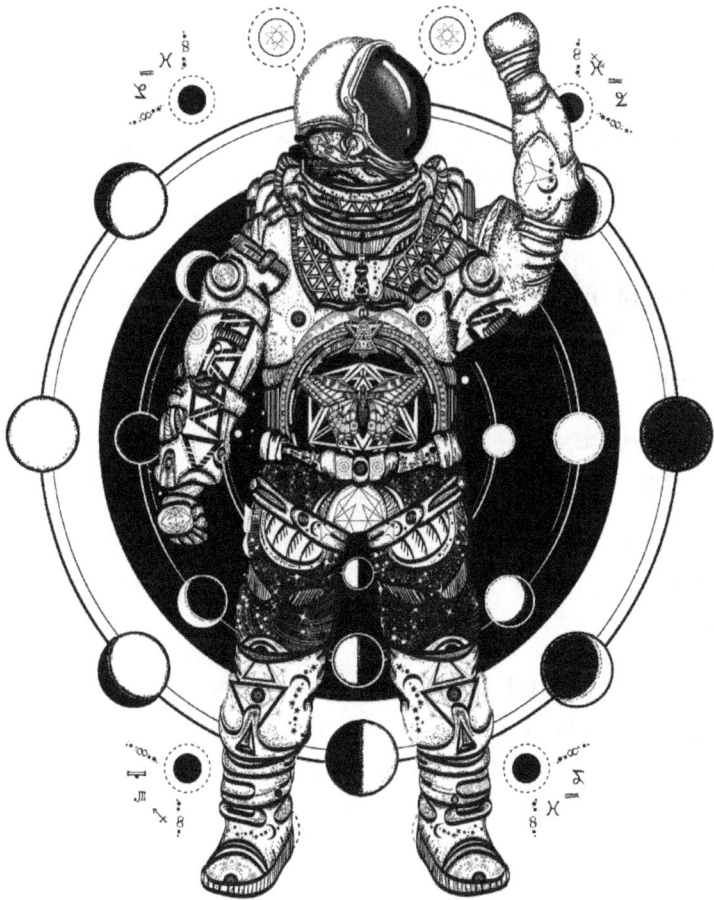

I had a lot of fun doing things that sort of collided with the world I grew up in.

I was gender fluid in style and sexuality. I was so lucky to be who I was, and I used this luck to push back on conforming to the status quo.

I dressed like a woman. I wore makeup. I had children with women, too. So the authorities of the world were constantly confused by me, and I was really happy doing that, the reason being that this brought me a lot of joy — taking on the status quo. You're doing this now, perhaps, even just reading this book.

The world needs change, and it needs love. I was able to find a way to lovingly change the world.

See? There's a difference between lovingly changing the world and trying to change it through violence.

I know that you sometimes need to push back aggressively. I learned that on the playground, but if you can do this with love, you will really have an idea of what kind of God you are, what kind of spiritual person you are, and what kind of wonderful creative being you are.

✦

Whatever you do, love yourself, then try to love the world. The reason I say "love yourself first" is, this is primary to your experience. This is not the same as loving just your body or your looks. This is about letting yourself fail sometimes without feeling like a loser.

Everybody loses sometimes, and this is a part of life. Don't feel that you need to win all the time. This is a mirage created by the system that tells you to perfectly correspond to what the world wants you doing, buying, and being. Don't give into this.

Love yourself, then try to love the world.

I was saying before how many times I've had to dial back my personas to enable me to be whole. I didn't give into any one persona until the end when I gave into my persona as a dying man. The Blackstar persona was somebody who wanted to feel better about the way death works—not on your schedule.

Death happens when you haven't made time for it.

I wished I could have kept going for another ten to twenty years. I hadn't considered I wouldn't until I was diagnosed with cancer. I wanted to plan how my life would end, of course. This would require an artistic representation of the tragedy that was in process.

Of course, for me it was a tragedy. I was not going to be whole until I came to terms with the fact that the tragedy was not really that: *it was just a change.* I had to focus on what I wanted to say, not on my grief.

There were times I would cry, and I would suffer knowing I would end my life without the kind of assurance of the afterlife that I have now. This was about the hardest thing for me, not knowing if I would continue. I know now, of course, that I would.

✦

But this was *not supposed to* be known by me.

In some ways, due to my large collection of books, I was open to this idea. This openness framed my final piece — *Blackstar* — which was an album of curses and chants and about the darkest kinds of projections of the afterlife I could envision. I was not going with a whole lot of dreams of fluffy clouds and angels. I wanted to penetrate the depth of feeling I had about leaving my world, and I think I was able to accomplish that very well.

Therefore, I had a means for expression that suited me. This helped my passage into the afterlife I'm in now. When I did, I was released from a lot of pain almost immediately — the body pain, that is.

Otherwise, there were things I had to work on. I had a lot of things that were never addressed: childhood things, murderous thoughts about people who crossed me sometimes, things like that. There were a lot of people, too, who took advantage of me without being straight about it.

These were things that were still bothering me. *Why did people do that?* This was the kind of question I had not yet resolved.

I learned through my own "repair shop" sort of building structure I went to, like you would go to a repair shop for a guitar or piano. That's the kind of world I created on the other side of your physical reality.

I was in a repair shop, and just as you might play a note on a piano or pluck a string on a guitar, the resonance from outside of my body made my body and soul move in sympathy with that sound.

It was like my body was potentiating the kind of nuanced healing of my mind and soul that I needed. It was terrific and so very moving that I had to move back for a while, past when I was supposed to leave that spot, just to enjoy the place of rest and relaxation I had encountered.

The way you might think of the afterlife, therefore, is a place where healing happens, but without any need to postpone this, because you have the ability to get healed on Earth, too, and I suggest you do this. There are countless therapies now just like mine, with sound healing, psychological healing, spiritual healing, water healing, animal communion kinds of things.

For every problem, there is an answer on your planet. I suggest that if you have any trouble whatsoever that you seek help.

There are always helpers—you know, *angels*—there with you, too.

This is something I learned while on the planet and I know this now, too.

STARMAN

The reason I chose to explore the dark side of dying was, of course, to show the transformation that the person in the *Blackstar* video went through.

The person expected nothing, then saw something. The something had hints of the old person he had been, a lost astronaut who would not be going home. The astronaut was found, the skull within his helmet decorated elaborately with jewels and transformative symbols that portrayed what I felt was about the most secret, personal, and mystical path one could take.

The path was as it was, the astronaut special to me. This was the gift of who I was: *the transpired self.*

With a wave of a wand, almost, the scents, sounds, tastes, everything came back to me, and I was surprised to see the colors were brighter. The colors, too, were many, beyond what you can see with your eyes.

The soul knows, though, about these colors.

The soul, as well, knows what path *you* need to be on for your own fulfillment. You're born with an intent in life that's far beyond what you might imagine. That's because the intent you were born with exists far beyond what you even imagine.

Your intent is about the best thing you could find, because your life has purpose, and your wonderful body and brain were created just for this purpose.

You don't have to know or be everything: *you just need to know and be what you need to know and be in order to live a happy life.*

✦

Beginning to believe that your life has purpose and a sort of direction is a good way to find out what that purpose is.

You know how I tried to be with others in ways that were fun? That's how you can try to be with others, too. To have fun with others will help you know what it is you think you want to do as a role in the world.

Everybody needs a role, I think, and the role will be something you enjoy doing, something you enjoyed doing even when you were a child.

This is something I did. All the signs were there. My putting myself on the street to fend for myself and sometimes getting into scrapes prepared me for the music world, full of the kinds of characters who want to bully you, but you need to be tough to stand up to.

I was musically inclined, too. I loved to sing and dance, and play with my friends in that sense, too. I had lovers who were very artistic, too, so this carried through in my adult years in different ways than my childhood allowed. I had a lot of people trying to find ways to be around me, so I was able to set boundaries well, which I learned as a child.

But even without all these things, whatever it is that you do well, these are things you can build on. If you were, for example, somebody who was shy as a child, not outgoing, you can find ways to be who you were then, perhaps as someone who enjoys doing things in more solitary ways.

Do you see? There are lots of options. The thing going forth is to realize you were born in the most fitting life for your soul to grow and enjoy itself.

These kinds of expressions will be different for everybody.

Just know these are all your soul's direction and **enjoy knowing there are reasons to follow what your soul calls to you to do.**

STARMAN

The exit strategy of mine, therefore, was about the best I could ever have accomplished.

I was able to sadly go forth, in a sense, without being maudlin, or overly concerned about my next life, or what would happen to me after I did.

I didn't need to say too many more goodbyes, as I had some years to do this. I was ready in every possible way I knew, and I was not going to do anything to stop it. There were reasons, I knew, for this to happen, and I sent myself along my path in ways that were beautiful.

I gave myself the gift of an anonymous funeral, in a sense. My funeral was somewhat of a pageant of anonymity, if you can believe that, because I wanted to just melt into the Earth having done everything I wanted to do.

While there were public celebrations, I really just wanted to be moving on without too much adulation about my accomplishments. I wanted to just go like everyman, having an everyman kind of experience. I was dead. End of story.

The next thing I knew, I was exalted, in a sense. I went from the plain, ordinary feeling about myself being buried or otherwise thrown as ashes into the winds. I was thinking this as I died, not knowing what to expect.

But the exaltation wasn't for *a rock star*: it was for a *human*.

Do you see? I was everyman, I was the exalted one, the same as every person ever born is going to be exalted in the sense of being shown appreciation for what they have done while living.

✦

This is something that takes a bit more explanation, but realize there are no bad actors in your world.

You have the kind of sense that the drama you are living is planned in some ways. The actors are those who you need to perform your own role in your own life. You are encumbered by many challenges, as every actor is. And you seek many answers from those around you.

This is because you're also living in sync with time, too, in a sense. In fact, you might think of everyone on the planet as playing a part of yourself in the world.

You are everyone. And everyone deserves to be exalted when they die, because that's how very special your time is on Earth as a soul in process, doing what you do every day.

You deserve to be exalted every day when you wake up and you decide to live the best life you can.

This is what happened to me. I let go of who I had been and became somebody bigger, but I wouldn't have been able to do this without foremost appreciating who I had been.

And this is true for everyone. This is what you can think of as your own appreciation for yourself. *You deserve to be loved, cared for, and to express your own inner light.*

When you do not feel loved, it's because of circumstances that help you know what this is like — to not be loved. Because as souls, you need to know this is something you don't want to feel, and you don't really want others to feel that way, either.

✦

I was something of a cad sometimes. I was somebody who'd love 'em and leave 'em and I wasn't always kind.

The reason it's important to know what we do to others when we hurt them is that we need to know what this is like, too, or we will never understand that our ability to empathize with people — to feel what they are feeling — is about the most important thing we can ever do.

And, this said, it's also important because we, as I mentioned earlier, are everyone who ever lived.

Now this may sound pretty far out. What you need to keep in mind is that there are many kinds of life in the stratosphere, and in completing one's life, the spiritual sense is engaged more than ever.

And what you realize is that to move beyond where you're at when you are nonphysical, you are required to feel people—other spirits—around you.

You have to have empathy to move beyond who you ever were into bigger areas of consciousness and expression.

You need to therefore learn—sooner than later, if you're lucky—that to love somebody, to feel for them, is about the most important thing in this world as well as beyond it.

There's no excuse to not learn to do this while you're alive. And in doing so, you will find about the best kind of life you can possibly imagine. Because when it comes right down to it, being loved and loving is about the best thing you can do—*ever*—in your physical world as well as beyond it.

There's nothing greater in the entire Universe than the power of love. Everything and everyone ever created been brought into being by love. Your world was created so everyone in it would be able to learn about this.

✦

Therapies here also include the kinds of remembrances that one had while physical.

You sometimes do this. You reminisce about good times you've had. This happens here, too. The thing to realize is, these *areas of love* — these *memories* — never go away.

Everything is conscious in your world, as well as far beyond it.

So the Universe and everything beyond it — in many lifetimes and spaces — all have the same kinds of rules about love.

That's why you sometimes have to say "this is why love works so well" because it's a constant in the Universe. And when you don't love, you really inhibit the flow of love in yourself.

And so when you love, you create, and when you create, you emulate whatever kind of Divine Self you want to be. But It is a Creator foremost, and It is loving and has a lot of cool projects going on everywhere all the time.

STARMAN

This is about the coolest thing you might imagine.

And of course the Universe, as I mentioned earlier, works through your creativity, too. Your creativity is about the best, most important part of your life. Whether or not you're ready to discover this is up to you.

This only takes a bit more strategy, perhaps, than you think it does. But to create something is about the coolest thing you can do, and the purpose of it is to allow yourself to enjoy yourself. This is the whole reason for doing it.

The real glory in art is self-satisfaction. And in this, you perpetuate the beauty of the Universe, which creates forever.

✦

The fundamentals, therefore, of life and love are that nothing ever dies. Everything exists in potential realties and in memories.

You don't ever have to feel that what you've lost has been lost forever: *you will catch up with it in time.*

The thing to realize is there are reasons for loss, and there's no telling what the loss is for, sometimes, until you responsibly grieve the loss. Because you never know what gifts will be found in grieving your loss. You will find many ways to go forward without what you have lost, and you will become new as a result.

So when you realize you've lost something, see this as a way to move beyond where you've been. Then go into a new space that's healthy for you. Don't sit around wanting what you lost to come back.

Do yourself a favor and learn from the loss, then let go and have an even better life without this thing or person. This is true in almost every case I know of.

Let go and trust that the reasons for loss are so you can become more whole.

Now, I want to talk a bit about my family because this was something of an odd thing.

I was born into a family perfectly suited to produce me, in some ways. Yet at the same time, there were challenges, things I wanted to overcome, the view of the world through the lens of suburbia being one. The sense that there were limitations to what people should do or not do was another.

The most terrifying aspect to my early life was the need to continually assure myself I was sane, as mental illness ran through my mother's side of the family and was a constant sorrow.

Finding myself as an artist, therefore, was in many ways a response to the ordered, sometimes fearful ways that my family had of responding to the world. I was able to see this as a perfect storm of a situation in which I would grow beyond. Then I did. I was able to put aside the emotional suffering that is the result of a hatred for oddness or any kind of unique ways of viewing the world.

This became a sharpened tool for me, this game of seeing what new ways of thinking I might enjoy taking part in, as well as what beauty I might bring that hadn't been done before.

✦

This is what I mean by turning a loss into a win. I realized early on that the way towards my own design for life was to sift through what I could and could not change, then sense what was not exactly a loss but an opportunity to consider things differently, which thrust me into the life I chose.

The sanity I gained from reading book after book after book propelled everything I did, and my works were informed by the best thinkers in the world.

If you are looking to move past your own circumstances, there are people who can help you find out where the gain is, rather than spending your days trying to get back something you lost or was never yours.

The characteristics of loss, therefore, are the same kinds of challenges that go along with any creative act.

You take what you have. You don't fret because you don't have all the art supplies that you wanted to make something. You just move forward, using your ingenuity to see where you might get inspiration, or more materials, or just work with what you have. You see the situation as a starting point, then you just keep going.

So do this. I have faith that you will turn out many wonderful, loving things and be fulfilled doing this. I really do.

✦

Painting is something I enjoyed, especially when I got older. This was about taking up the time I had while older that otherwise would have been spent on activities that helped my family and career. At the end of my life, I had more time to spend on these kinds of pursuits.

The trouble was, I didn't really care as much about the painting as I did the suffering of the artist who never had the chance to see his works in the world as a successful way to gauge his artistry.

I wasn't really having much fun knowing that the art I did was going to be successful in the world of art because by then I had made a name for myself as an artist, actor, musician.

I wanted to do things for myself. I still had a nagging feeling, though, about how many people do their art without anyone really appreciating them. I have this feeling still, which has to do with why I wanted to write this book.

✦

You see, I don't want you to have the problem of being a suffering artist.

For one thing, you don't need to suffer to do art. This is something that's perhaps the most fundamental flaw in people's minds about being an artist. As I said earlier, you just need to use what's available to you, do your best, then share it in some ways.

The reason the world is so full of frustrated people is because the world has used this lie to perpetuate the idea that there shouldn't be artists. The world is fearful. Thinking about doing something like this is thought to be another kind of folly, like having a soft spot for people, or having some kind of disability to do anything grand.

Don't believe these things. The world needs people in it doing all kinds of lovely works of art that heal people and bring people together.

When you think about art, you sometimes get the feeling that the art around these days is not as good as when the masters like Raphael or Michelangelo were alive. This isn't really true, though.

While it can help to have technique and form that's practiced, you can do art any way you feel like. This is about the purest way to live. The way to consider formulating a way to paint, for example, can sometimes depend on learning more about artists' techniques.

And I would say this applies, too, to music and anything else that you would like to pursue artistically. Learn from others living and dead, and you will gain so much in how you approach your work, too, because they have millions of things to share with you, too. The reasons for doing art, therefore, aren't to make a fortune or to make a name for yourself.

The reasons for doing art are to enjoy yourself, to shed light on what you feel, and to express yourself in ways that connect with others.

That's all. Then, if you're lucky, and you have a sense the purpose of your life is to pursue your craft, do so. Get better at the work and you'll find before you know it that you're living your best life.

STARMAN

The purpose of my life, therefore, was to make art, but also to tend to those I loved.

I had a very big heart towards the friends I was able to enjoy in my life. These were often collaborators, which is about the best way to do your work, because having people around you is really the point.

The surface level effects of my rock star life are that I was the figurehead, in a sense. But these works wouldn't have happened without the thoughts and talents of those I loved: my family, my collaborators. My audience, too, was a huge part of my works.

The characters were helpful, too. When I slipped into the persona of Ziggy Stardust, for example, I was able to tap into the sorts of feelings that he had to enable the projection for what a rock star would be, then I became that.

✦

The pressures of the music industry were easier to take, too, when surrounded by friendly people, so this was not something to take lightly. The music industry has always been notoriously cutthroat and not worth it for some people. Having allies helped.

The dedication, therefore, of others, goes a long way in figuring out where you want to go with your life.

The spectacles were the result of thousands of hours of planning, designing, producing — so much that the spectacles themselves were the works of art they needed to be for those who created them.

This is another kind of artistry that has a lot of power to make or break rock stars and is worth its weight in gold when setting out to entertain people. We — together — realized a kind of Heaven on Earth when audiences came to spend time with us. These were like the holiest places on Earth for me and I still feel that way now.

✦

The patterns of life that I see now have a lot to do with how you want to express the holy in your life.

This isn't the same as the churches you grew up with, necessarily, though it could be. The sanctity of a church, mosque, temple, cathedral — anywhere that people gather together to express their solidarity and love for each other — is holy.

There are other kinds of gathering spaces that, for me, were the best. These were the kinds of concerts that I starred in but were supported by armies of people expressing their own creativity, too. So these were awesome experiences that were also transcendent.

That's what I'd like to talk about now: how very transcendent some of the world is when you really think about it.

The world has lots of places where you can feel better. These may be art museums, schools, works of enterprise that feel right to you such as city squares or monuments to those who have done heroic deeds. They may be beautiful buildings, such as cathedrals, or new kinds of living spaces. They might be lands that are special to you, such as beaches, forests, farms, and mountains.

The fact is, almost everywhere you go is holy. You just don't think of it that way.

The bombarded spaces of war-torn countries are examples. Here you have the worst evil in the world causing the suffering of many individuals. The places are still holy, though. You just may not think of them this way.

So when you concern yourself with reestablishing holy places with the sense of dignity and sanctity that you might when attending a church, you will see what's really going on: that whatever has occurred to the places that are suffering, these are still places that are holy.

And your ability to see them this way is important. Why? Because they exist for you to *see*. They exist for you to *feel*. They exist for you to *see as needing to be healed*, that's all.

In doing this, you can also see the places in yourself that are holy and need to be healed.

You can see the places in your mind that you have thought things that were not worthy of you as being healed. You can sense that the world really does want to be better.

But the suffering is part of it. This is because the world is you — *all of it* — regardless of how you may think of it.

When you pause to see the world as suffering, and your brothers and sisters perishing in the world's worst places, you will understand that the world needs you in it trying your best to exert your best energy and direction towards being whole and helping others as best as you can. You'll see yourself as the kind of person who is open to the world in ways that are beautiful, and you will see that the world is needing you *in* it, not just as an observer, but as a human being who cares, that's all.

The purpose of letting go of what you think of as being a holy place and embracing *everywhere* as a holy place will help you see the world is fraught with many kinds of angels—those who suffer, those who help, those who cause conflict.

This is purposeful. What you're learning to do is to shut out what you see as not helpful and move into the space where you can thrive. In doing this, you will be whole in ways that are remarkable. You will sense things happening to you that you've never understood as possible.

The purpose of your life, therefore, is to experience it without the need to feel the world isn't on your side, because it is.

The world is on your side, always.

I did a lot of changing in my life. I wasn't the kind of person you might think had a lot of changes that were fun, either. The attire, the attitude, were all conveniently displayed onstage as the sorts of characters who had something to say. This was wonderful to do. However, these weren't the only kinds of changes I needed to make.

The suffering of the world has to do with the reality that every change somebody needs to make takes a lot of effort sometimes. This was the same for me. The fact that I was a superstar didn't absolve me from anything I needed to look at, things that I was able to see as ways I needed to change.

The way, sometimes, that film stars or other celebrities have of being in the spotlight while having a rough time has to do with the difficulty that every human being takes on when they decide to *be* human beings. It's as if the world gives us the proper kind of education required to be whole in the sense of our own soul, or whatever you want to call it — our absolutely best Self, you might say.

This has to do with the kinds of experiences we all have beyond this world. I am here to tell you this exists, too.

However, for now let's just take a few breaths and figure out more about changes together, shall we?

The path for you has been about the best kind of path that you could experience given how you wanted to be in the world as a soul in process.

This means that the characteristics of how you decided to look, where you were able to be born, what you chose as a life ahead, these are all—weird as it sounds—completely chosen by who you are on a higher plane.

You chose the kinds of experiences you wanted to have so you can learn to be whole in new ways—in *soulful* ways—without needing to ever feel like this was some kind of betrayal or punishment.

I don't see this as a betrayal or punishment. I see this as an accomplishment of about the best kind, the wonderful world of soul.

This is how you can think about your life: as being totally purposeful without needing to feel like you have to accomplish some huge purpose. This is more about having a sense you're exactly where you need to be now, and you will move into other experiences when you feel like it.

This is a wonderful way to consider the many forms of expressing themselves that people do. This is why, also, you can trust that when you consider yourself as being here in a way that's very purposeful, you will feel better about yourself and your expressions will be better, too. They will be more fun, loving, and great in the sense of performing as a human being really should, as another kind of loving person in the world.

Taking your frustrations out on someone, therefore, isn't going to help anybody, it'll only hurt them, and to take responsibility for yourself is how you can stop being miserable sometimes.

The idea here is that every trend, every change, every event has in it the seeds of some kind of beauty that will lead you into the kinds of changes you need, and this will be how you will love and grow throughout your life.

In other words, changes really are needed all the time. Getting used to change will help you immensely.

✦

Here's how I did it. When I was afraid, I told somebody. I told a friend or lover. Then I was able to find ways to let go of my fears because my findings in discussing things with my friend would lead me into scenarios as to how I might not fear this thing anymore.

Sometimes it was simply a matter of seeing that this thing wasn't worth my time in being fearful of it. This sometimes allowed more fun instead of fear.

Sometimes I needed to realize I didn't need to worry about something because it wasn't in my control anyway. I sought out ways to address my fears, and I wasn't always great at this because this isn't as easy as it may sound.

Sometimes I went too far towards one way and said, "I'm going to give everything I can to *this*," or I said, "I'm going to give nothing to *that*," when the real-life scenarios actually called on me to find a middle way towards resolving conflicts and such.

✦

You can do this, too. The facts remain that the body is as wonderful as it can be, right? This isn't just a random thought here, so bear with me.

The body is about as fine an instrument as anything. So why would you encourage your body to go anywhere that isn't safe, or be around anyone but loving people? So many of my friends were able to help me do that by saying, "This person isn't good for you," or "This lesson is about not being the same person you think you have to be."

Therefore, the kinds of changes I went through were all about having a sort of grace-filled transition into something better for me. This was about the best thing I could do, of course. My friends helped me.

If you don't have somebody to talk to, like a wise friend, you can find support in other ways, through a counselor or some other guide who can show you a better way to think about the things you feel fearful about.

This is something that I had options for, and you will, too, when you look into this online or in person where you live.

I can't stress this strongly enough because getting used to change is about the best thing you can do.

This is because **changes never, ever go away**. They are always waiting around the next bend to tell you what's best for you.

Changes never ever go away

I receive a lot of "indirect messages" from people in physical reality that I sometimes respond to. When I say "indirect," I mean these are sometimes coded as thoughts about me without being the kind of direct messages as in, "Hey, David, will you please turn on the radio for me?"

This has to do with how very connected everybody is in the world you live in, as well as the world I now inhabit. The spiritual world has all of us connected—each person who ever lived—and therefore you can feel better about everything, knowing you have a lot of friends in your world and beyond it.

There's no reason to believe you need to check out to transcend your world. You can connect with us here anytime.

This is what I mean by our own connection with each other. It's like a kind of string plucked in the guitar shop I mentioned earlier. There are frequencies related to each person who ever lived, and so we resonate greatly when we're feeling this way or that.

Consider how deeply you miss people sometimes—those who are not physical anymore.

Perhaps you've lost grandparents or even parents, siblings, or friends.

The loss you feel is real and there's reason to feel what you feel. You grow not by suffering but by finding ways to *love differently*. One of the reasons I say "love differently" is that they still exist in your thoughts, and they are able to reach you through your own understanding of how you feel about them.

This is a sort of harmonic that I described earlier as frequencies. You can tune into your loved ones to feel them with you, and you might even receive some advice from them if you ask for it. They want to help.

✦

Therefore, I'm with you now in the writing of this book, and I can be reached, too, in your thoughts. I will always be sending loving thoughts regardless if I get your indirect message or not.

That's just how the world works. I have no appointments to keep because there are no boundaries like the kinds of time and space boundaries you have on your planet. There are no limits to my world or to the way spirit flows through everything. So you don't ever have to think that I'm unavailable. I'm with you whenever you'd like.

The thoughts are necessary for yourself only, really. You need to sometimes transmit the thoughts you have into the stratosphere and see where they go, too. As I said earlier, you create your reality, so focusing on positive outcomes is important.

This is something of a wonderful new way to consider what you can do to change how you think about things, because when you commit to doing some things differently, and then say, "I'm going to do this with this thing, I'm going to see where this goes," you help create that in your life.

So focusing on what you want to do or see will be super helpful as you move through your days.

Beyond anything else, your thoughts create the kinds of worlds you want to see, and this is where I'm at, too, in a sense.

Starman

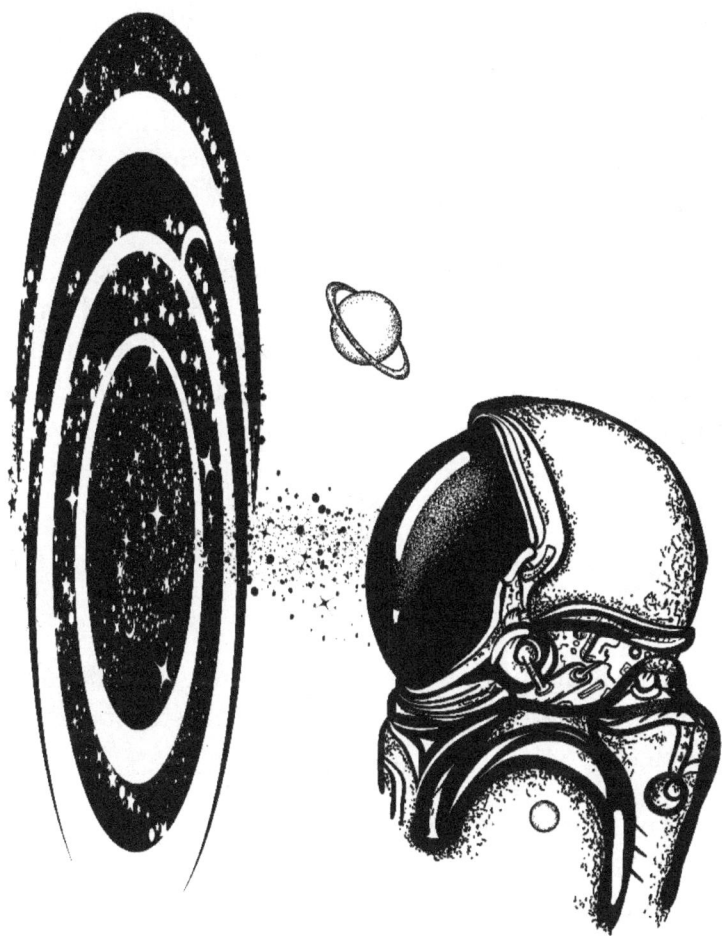

I'm where I wanted to be, in a space of fun and love with everybody around me who I love.

This is what awaits you, too. However, there's purpose, as I said, to your life, and it's important to continue towards your own destinations without wanting to get here too soon.

The world, therefore, is an amazing place, full of magic and music. The thrilling life I led had everything to do with music and I will talk about the special things about music now because I think this is important.

✦

There's nothing more spiritual than music.

This is about the best way you can grow through anything that life throws at you: to listen to good music.

The world gives you all kinds of music to choose from: beatbox grooves, to piccadilly rhymes, to ultra-rich orchestrations, to the music of the spheres.

Music will move you in ways that no angels ever did. And this is why music is something of a miracle. It is your best way of getting the feeling of what the holiest things are in life.

This has to do with the fact that music exists in a sort of midway space between spiritual worlds and your own physical world.

*

The *music of the spheres* is about the best choice you can make, because it's about how the world moves, really.

This has been ignored by many people without any regard to its importance, but the music of the spheres captures the world in its embrace all the time, you just need to have the sounds come through you in ways you don't yet, perhaps.

When you listen to music, try to hear the music of the spheres in it — *the music of the movement of celestial bodies*. This will always be there. Sometimes the choice of music can help, but ultimately the music of the spheres is always embedded.

You need to, foremost, *feel into* the music, then breathe and meditate a bit, then you will feel wonderful. That's all.

This is about the best kind of thing you can do for yourself because this truly is sacred and necessary for love and life.

The reason I say this so emphatically — suggesting that you listen to the music of the spheres — is because this is about the best way to heal, too.

The kinds of auditory sensations you get when listening to music are another way to heal than perhaps you've been taught. Your brain loves good music. Your mind is built to include good music in its development.

The reason is that their subtle frequencies include healing tones that potentiate the kinds of frequencies that your mind matter requires to heal and grow. This has been thoroughly studied and you can find the research on your own.

The pedagogical underpinnings of music also help to create empathy of "soul to soul" that teaches children how to be with others in ways standard learning cannot.

The music of nursery rhymes also helps children learn the basic structures of storytelling, something deeply inherent and necessary in terms of development as human beings.

The storytelling that music brings reaches into the kinds of cultural explorations that every great classroom has in it. Incorporating other cultures' music teaches great things about other cultures, and even the development of one's own culture.

✦

The joys of music shared are rife with ways to increase unity.

Dancing extends music into feelings that are expressed through the body, perhaps the only way to really liven up any gathering and get people really digging each other.

Singing traditional songs together raises one's ability to offer to others the kind of kinship required to form strong relationships. The wedding songs, the church songs, the prayers, the fashionable songs: every song has some quality of finding unity between people and calming and healing souls.

Singing together brings a "heart math," as they call it, to bear to bring peace to those human body elements, too.

So the studious person will put on music to study with, the composer will listen to other composers to find their own soul tone, the brain will adapt to miraculous ways of healing, the body will, as well, respond to the kinds of healing brought on by the use of tonal frequencies to attend to specific ailments.

The reasons, therefore, for studying, playing, singing, dancing — and everything you might ever imagine — with music are full of potential to provide, in the coming centuries in your development as a culture, the very elements you require to heal and transcend the situation you're in now.

Don't pass up any opportunity to listen to every kind of music.

They all have something you can learn from and grow into.

I had the kind of embrace for music as a child that I had when I went from physical to nonphysical, and I started on my way with the same kinds of music I was able to produce in my final days.

The song about the Blackstar was the kind of feeling I had when I passed, then it changed into the kind of sonorous music of the spheres I needed to hear.

Along my journey, the music changed into a kind of experience of being at one with everything, embraced by the sounds of the spheres.

And I listened with my feelings—my *internal* feelings—in the sense of feeling like I was it, this Oneness. *I was it, too.*

The music moved beyond the kind of attention I gave myself when physical into the kind of lounge space where I would sometimes rest in my home.

The music was with me then, and I was able to discard there the worries I had, because I was One now with Everything. I knew everything was as it was supposed to be.

I didn't worry about how I had been while on Earth. I was able to be whole without doing much more than sort more out than I was able to on Earth. In this, the granting of humility was something I found deep joy in, how I had been granted a kind of humility to bear with honor what I had taken on.

✦

The only things I had to sort through had to do with the way in which I had sometimes wondered, *why do people do that?* This had caused me suffering. Surely they must know better than to cause so much suffering to others.

What I was able to see was that the people who cause so much harm really don't know what they're doing half the time. They are persecuting themselves, then they take it out on others. This has to change to make the world a better place.

So what I learned more than I had when on Earth was that *the spiritual realm really does what it can to help the world.*

Sometimes, though, it requires humans to take responsibility for their actions, and to do this you sometimes need to call people on their actions, to hold them accountable. Because living in ignorance isn't healthy for anyone, even those who are ignorant.

So when you can, without needing to use force, try to hold others accountable for their actions. This can really make a difference because as you know, you get better, too, when somebody says you can do better.

This is why I say this is needed: you wouldn't be the person you are now if your parents or other loving authority hadn't sometimes told you this, right?

So be the person you need to be and help others be who they need to be. This is really needed in the world.

✦

The suffering of the world, therefore, is communicated to us through our senses.

We know what's going on. We know what you suffer with, too. Therefore, we continually lend energy to you in order to help you through your changes.

This is what we will always do.

The way we help you, therefore, is *through your senses*. You can feel us near you whenever you think differently about what you may have been brought up to believe.

The psychic impressions you have about who you *have been* in this reality, and who you *may become* in this reality, are shaped by your insights about what exactly this moment holds for you.

Does this moment hold promise of beautiful things, or do you hear yourself thinking, "This is not what I want"?

This is something of a trick question, though, because wanting things that you don't really need or desire will be always trying to get your attention. This is why I say to expect the kind of beauty in each moment that you feel is possible.

This will bring you to the kind of feeling space that we—us angels here—exist in now. When I say "we," it's just because I'm more than who I was while on Earth. I've shifted into an older gentleman kind of angel, a collection of who I was then and who I have become.

The world never ceases to amaze me, still, and the reason I say this is I'm still the human I was while on Earth, too.

I'm everything I've ever thought or expected to be. I'm every person I've been while on Earth. I've moved through so much experience that I've become improved, but also still have all these selves connected into a kind of gestalt of who I have ever been or will be.

This is because—why wouldn't I want to be something of a wide person with so many wonderful experiences to draw from?

And when you really think about this, why wouldn't anybody including you—why wouldn't *you*—eventually want to become part of a larger Selfhood to connect with all the many aspects of yourself that you have ever wanted to be?

This isn't so much about trying to feel *better* as much as it is to feel *whole*. You don't need to put on any airs about what you think you want to be because you're already there now, with us.

In this, you have a greater Self who loves you, knows you, and is eternally potentiating everything you've ever wanted to be.

How's that for a perspective on who you really are? This is why I say *you're a Starman, too. You just don't realize it yet!*

The fact remains that the Universe is big, beyond compare with anything you've ever imagined.

And this is something of a perpetual challenge for anybody who ever lived to consider: that the world continues to evolve and goes beyond where you may not ever have imagined into realms of understanding and chaos and lots of different ways to express oneself, beyond really anything you could dream of.

The fact is, too, that you've dreamed of your life now. What better way to consider your ability to move through this life than as moving through a dream that's real?

It's wonderful, really, to consider the world this way, and practical, too, because dreams have wonderful depth to them. There are encoded messages in each dream, in fact.

You might have fun looking for the kinds of similar things I liked to think about: synchronicities, messages from spacemen, all kinds of wonderful magic that eludes people who don't see what I'm describing now — the kind of soulless perspectives that make the world dry and ordinary.

This is not what the world is about. But to see the world for what it is, you need ample provisions of love, acceptance, the glorious feeling of connection, the attitude of humility, and the gratitude with which you say each day, "I'm glad to be alive."

I'm not indicating that sometimes you won't have bad days. These are part of life. I'm saying that typifying your world as beautiful has merits to it.

You can change your world for the better just by allowing these thoughts into your thinking—that your life is magical, that you have many reasons to dream what you want to create, the reality you desire, and to allow yourself to feel the world is on your side.

The world is not only on your side—it's full of messages to you that you can take note of to see what might be happening deep inside you.

Your dreams come from your very Source, and you can find ways to get help in translating what you dream about. You might find a friend you can trust to share them with, and consider their suggestions, but however you choose to translate your dreams is up to you.

Try to keep an open, positive mind and you will learn to invoke the kinds of dreams and reality you desire.

Remember Dreams

The way towards the bright future that awaits you, therefore, has more to do with the perspective I'm sharing with you now than any kind of thing you might think you need or want in the world.

The reasons for living are beyond those things, really, and beyond the kinds of silly mischief some people want to thrust on you. Don't let them. Try to have fun throughout your days and you will have numerous people around you who love you and want you to be having a good life. That's all.

The way to consider what you do each day to help the world is what you can think of as the things that bring you joy.

There's no reason to think that helping others was ever intended to be something that you necessarily had to suffer to do. The suffering happens sometimes, and this is because people really do sometimes have to serve in ways that require a sort of sacrifice. This is what makes humans great, this ability to sometimes put aside one's own fears to do something to help somebody.

This is what you might think of as sometimes needed, but not always. What really is needed is for people who *have the capacity* to do clever, fun things —with the kind of spirit that I had—to *do* those things. And that requires a sense of one's personal direction and joy.

✦

If you remember being in secondary school — or high school, depending on your locale, and perhaps you still are there now — you have a sense that the forming of groups is tantamount to the culture. You form groups of sports people, music people, theatre people, nerdy people, which I was one of in some ways.

Then you sometimes have those on the outskirts of the groups who don't really want to be part of a group or aren't wanted by the group. That's because this person might see things differently. That was me, too.

This is not to say the groups are wrong, they sometimes just don't have a lot going on beyond the superficial ideas that most high schoolers tend to dream about.

This is why some people who go through school as loners tend to be really great people when they are older. They have learned to pursue the kinds of things that bring them joy.

This is something I want you to consider: to find the things you want to do to bring yourself joy, then to bring that joy to the world, including the people you care about most.

You don't have to make a big splash. You don't have to make a lot of money. You just need to find the things you're interested in. Eventually these things will become passions to pursue when you get out of high school, perhaps, or even before.

This is about the best thing you can do to have a genius life, because you will then be able to commit to something steadily.

A form of discipline is good for this, to make your way in the world with something to offer. Discipline isn't the bad word that some have sought to make it, meaning some sort of punishment. Discipline is dedicating yourself to learning something as well as practicing so you can get good at it.

This brings you into the proximity to others who will be close friends, partners, and colleagues — the kind I had in my day.

This is the best thing you might do, for the purpose of life really is to enjoy it, then try to bring your presents — and presence — to the world.

The thing to keep in mind when you're a teenager is that the brain is only about three quarters finished developing, while the body is going forward trying to get laid or trying to figure out what's going on in the first place. Your teen years are about the best time to try things if you can do so safely. Because — remember — *your brain is not finished yet.*

The way to consider this is to postpone anything that may seem odd or dangerous until you are a grownup. This is to say anything that will put you in danger needs to not happen when you are a teenager.

You would be better suited for finding a way to exercise your hormonal energy in ways that are productive, like joining a theatre group or starting a band or doing things with the friends you have that are fun.

This doesn't mean being irresponsible. This means having fun safely.

✦

This said, sex is a big deal when one is a teenager. What some people miss about sex is that the sex can be wonderful when you're a teenager, but it can also be *not* wonderful.

Doing things that are not violations of others, that are respectful, that are responsible in the sense of prevention of disease and pregnancy, are all good for people. Don't give into the idea that you have to score with a lot of people, though, or to be ashamed.

People need to know the facts: that children should not have sex, but teenagers need it, and if you can't get laid, then do this for yourself.

Learn to be responsible sexually with yourself, too, and it's healthy to find release on your own.

This is not a contest for finding ways to show anybody what you may think you have to. You just need to be respectful towards yourself and others.

Your sexuality is a Divine gift, fully blessed with wondrousness.

Allow yourself to enjoy it responsibly and with gratitude for yourself and others.

Now, sex, drugs, and rock and roll can be the best things to consider for how your world needs to progress.

The facts are that loving who you want to love, having fun, dancing, and listening to music are the about the best things there are to establish common ground with people. These can be enjoying rock concerts, or small gatherings of people hanging out in clubs where people listen to music and dance.

Everything you might consider healthy can be cast into the form of sex, drugs, and rock and roll. Let me explain.

The sexual revolution was charted in the fifties, expressed in the sixties, became toxic in the seventies, was repressed in the eighties, was ignored in the nineties, was claimed again in the twenty-first century, often in the form of freedom of love between people of every kind.

The wax and wane of the sexual revolution was all about how committed we were to expression—*real* human expression—not what you buy in stores, not what you sell on the market. What you see now is the packaging of sexuality in ways that will not be counted on in the future as the best ways, because the packaged sexuality you see now really isn't about self-expression or love, it's about selling records or what have you.

Now, I was one of the people who may have had something to do with this. I was also somebody who used my sexual self as a representation of a culture that was in need of being seen. Therefore, I feel mine was different. I was exposing a need for people to be seen, not exposing the current thinking about what will sell.

So in your expressions about who needs to be seen and heard, you can count on the fact that there will always be other people who need to be seen and heard, who have a lot to give, and who need you to support them.

And you will find yourself being one of those people, too, sometimes, as you begin to shed the ideas that you have been entrained with that you need to have *things* to be successful, that you need to go work at *jobs you hate*, that you need to find ways to *always* be cheerful. But this will not be the path for those who know deep down what they need to express and do so.

This will not be the same for everybody. This is all about *personal* expression with regard to what *you feel* needs to be shared. This is about the best thing to look forward to, as people all over the world will be embracing the kind of soulful intent that I've described earlier.

With this comes responsibility, of course. Expression has two sides to it: the expression that's healthy and expression that's not. Be healthy!

✦

Now, we here on the other side of the stars have another bone to pick with the capitalistic ways of the world and that is its tendency to prescribe exactly what is right and wrong for everybody without the best of intentions behind it.

The mirror of Selfhood has a way of showing you what you need to see as right or wrong.

This requires a firm grasp of your own moral intuition. See this as a way to sort out things as you go, not as a tool to beat people with, but a tool to help you say and do things that are congruent with the health and well-being of the planet and all of its creatures.

All forms of life need your love and compassion.

This goes right back to the idea of sex drugs and rock and roll, too.

Because when you are able to break with the kinds of repressive hierarchies in the world today and move into a state of freedom and personal responsibility, you will see that the world really needs you to do things differently, perhaps, than how you were brought up.

You can sort those things out for yourself, but mostly these have to do with sharing your food with your brothers and sisters around the world.

This is where rock and roll comes in, too, because the best thing about rock and roll is that it welcomes all into its embrace, and *all people around the world benefit when rock and roll comes to town.*

✦

The drug part is the one to watch out for. The recreational drugs that can benefit come with a warning to make sure you remain healthy and wise, not as a druggie or junkie who uses them to remove themselves from the world.

There are also dangers that go with the terrible ways in which people try to destroy each other through the false packaging of drugs that kill people. Avoid these, of course.

The way to consider drugs, therefore, is as potential helpers, tools to help you heal or have some insights, not to be mindless about, not to be irresponsible with.

The prayers you say when you go to sleep are basically the same ways to connect you with your greater Self as any drug you take will ever do.

Therefore, stay with the kinds of medicines you know to be safe, mostly things that are found in Nature, and you will find a balance in the sense of having medicines on hand, not ways to escape or to put aside your worries.

✦

This said, the climate of social change will be unfettered soon enough as more individuals are able to heal from the trauma of the world and the hangups that many adults in charge have.

This is not to say the persons in charge of governments are necessarily wrong, they aren't. Closely watched governments are a good thing, and individuals who exercise their civil rights and the duties of responsible citizenry will be necessary to move your world forward.

Don't hesitate to run for office in local or other kinds of elections. Governments are required for the smooth running of shared interests, meaning those that are good for people, *all* people.

Be aware of what's going on in your neighborhoods, your country, your world, because the time has come for people to not bury their heads in the sand with regard to what is happening around them.

You need to be informed. Do that.

The options I had as a child were so very narrow it's amazing that I was able to move beyond what I knew then.

I was able to see how disinterested the neighborhood was with regard to societal events, cultural statements, the historic underpinnings of what was happening in the world, the psychology of humans, the philosophies at work in the world, some working well in it, others totally destroying it, so I learned quickly to be more informed than most.

Then I set out to find things I enjoyed. Then I worked hard to make myself something of a steward of the odd person, a sort of chameleon to express what was needing to be expressed.

In other words, *I found my own way to be cool.* I knew deep down that dressing like everyone else, talking like everyone else—doing things to fit in— was not cool. It was in every way the antithesis of what I thought was cool and still do. Because being cool isn't doing things because your peers are. Being cool is not thinking that you're better or more aloof than everyone else. Being cool isn't even a fashion statement.

Being cool is expressing your most authentic self and being okay with it.

This has to do with having respect for yourself and others and is the lifeblood of the world. Being cool is about the best thing to try to achieve, only not in the ways you've been taught.

Don't try to fit in. Try to be guided by where you need to be, then go forth with the air of dignity that you deserve while being respectful of yourself and others.

What kind of clothes suit you best? What kinds of food keep you healthiest? What forms of artistry are you stirred by? What is it in you that you want to express? What is fun for you? What are you good at, and what skills can you learn to help you with your life? These questions are about the most important ones you can ask because life really doesn't get any more basic than that.

STARMAN

Skills are necessary to get you into a flow of life where you can then build upon them in ways that you enjoy. So learning a trade or basic discipline — as I did as a musician — is *about finding your way in the world without needing to worry too much about being reliant to the degree that you have to alter yourself to meet somebody else's wishes for you.*

In other words, you need to find ways to be responsible and autonomous and not require anyone to tell you what to do.

This will all be the result of learning what is right for you.

That's the coolest thing you can do: to be yourself.

STARMAN

The way I thought things would go is, I would become a movie star, eventually, then give up music. This is not the way it went, though. I did many movies. This was just not the path that I thought it was.

This will happen to you, too. You'll see how you might move forward then change direction, sometimes, along the way. There's no need to be narrow-minded about what you will do or be.

Things go along as they need to, and that's how they were for me. I was able to morph into so many different characters that I had to sometimes take a breather to see who I was beneath all of them. This was a sort of state of composure that took me into beautiful places, too, and new countries of thinking.

I read a lot of philosophy and commentary about the world, and was able to use these things for my own benefit, too. I helped the world by being knowledgeable about it to the degree that I found a presence in myself.

This is a good thing, too, to just allow yourself to be who you are. It's something of an odd thing to say, perhaps, but knowing who you have become, knowing your faults, knowing what the world expects of you, knowing what you can give but sometimes push back on — these are all things that you need in order to feel better about everything.

You just need to sometimes feel better about things.

And in those moments, we have a lot of interest — we angels — because we like to drop in to share our thoughts with you, too. Big thoughts, higher thoughts that you might think of as inspiration. This is our job, just as you're finding in reading this book now.

We take our time and come around to you when you might not even expect it. So let go of thinking that there's nobody around to help and love you sometimes. There are always those like us around you, helping you each day with the kind of whispers of words or thoughts that you may think are miraculous... *and they are.*

And what a world you've chosen to be part of! What a world it is, having seen so many bad days and now it looks forward to something greater. Be the kind of change you wish to see in the world. Begin with yourself and you will see clearly how to be in it. We angels trust that you will.

With love and best wishes for a beautiful life,

Starman

ABOUT THE AUTHOR

Joanne Helfrich is an author and channeler whose works promote personal and collective transformation. With the essence of Rose, she provides guidance to help individuals know and embrace their soul's design for expression and fulfillment. She lives in Topanga, California, with her husband and collaborator, Paul M. Helfrich. For more information, visit joannehelfrich.com.

Other books by Joanne Helfrich

The Way of Spirit:
Teachings of Rose

The Afterlife of J.D. Salinger:
A Beautiful Message from Beyond

Let That Shit Go:
Learn to Process Loss and Be Happy

Afterlives: Firsthand Accounts
of Twenty Notable People

www.ingramcontent.com/pod-product-compliance
Lightning Source LLC
Chambersburg PA
CBHW031554040426
42452CB00006B/305